INSPIRE ME
A Book of
Odes and Things

INSPIRE ME
A Book of Odes and Things

P.D. MEADE

ASA PUBLISHING CORPORATION
AN INNOVATIVE OUTSOURCE BOOK PUBLISHING HYBRID

ASA Publishing Corporation
29 S. Monroe, St., Suite 201, Monroe, Michigan 48161
An Accredited Publishing House with the BBB
www.asapublishingcorporation.com

All Rights Reserved. No part of this publication may be reproduced, stored in a retrieval system or transmitted in any form or by any means electronic, mechanical, photocopying, recording or otherwise, without the prior written permission of the publisher. Author/writer rights to "Freedom of Speech" protected by and with the "1st Amendment" of the Constitution of the United States of America. This is a work of non-fiction; poetry. Any resemblance to actual events, locales, person living or deceased that is not related to the author's literacy is entirely coincidental.

With this title/copyrights page, the reader is notified that the publisher does not assume, and expressly disclaims any obligation to obtain and/or include any other information other than that provided by the author except with permission. Any belief system, promotional motivations, including but not limited to the use of non-fictional/fictional characters and/or characteristics of this book, are within the boundaries of the author's own creativity in order to reflect the nature and concept of the book. Unless otherwise indicated, most scripture quotations are taken from the King James Version of the Bible.

Any and all vending sales and distribution not permitted without full book cover and this copyrights page.

Copyrights©2023, P. D. Meade, All Rights Reserved
Book Title: Inspire Me *A Book of Odes and Things*
Date Published: 03.19.2023
Book ID: ASAPCID2380857
Edition: 1 *Trade Paperback*
ISBN: 978-1-960104-06-9
Library of Congress Cataloging-in-Publication Data

This book was published in the United States of America.
Great State of Michigan

Table of Contents

Do Not Worry 1

Introduction 5

What's In Your Spiritual Wallet? 10

Prayer Is The Key That Unlocks All Doors! 11

Internalized 12

The Emperor's New Clothes 14

Victorious Life 15

What Do You Live By? 16

The Tabernacle is Not Just A Building 17

Family First 20

Praise Break 21

B.F.L.I.E.V.E. 22

What's Going On? 24

Fear Not 26

Where To Go For Your Prayer Needs 29

Essential Living 33

Old Chinese Proverbs 35

You Count! 37

Nothing Heals If You Make It Fester 38

Redemption 39

Forgiveness 40

- Difficult Circumstances Releases Courage 43
- L.O.V.E. 44
- Dear Family 45
- Special Words.. 46
- Bless Yourself 48
- I Am Blessed 49
- Playing For Keeps 50
- Sweet Honesty 52
- What A Surprise 54
- Destiny 55
- Jamaica... 56
- Someone Like You 57
- Man Of My Dreams 58
- Imagine... 59
- God Is Real 60
- Prayer For The World... 61
- So True 61
- No Time For God? 62
- God Without Man Is Still God! 62
- Something 62
- This is Who We Are 63
- Be Educated 63
- Where Are You Going?... 63

Who Matters?	64
Stop!!!	65
No What?	65
A Little Tidbit . . . Enjoy!	66
Overwhelming Grace	67
Impacted Journey	68
Make It Now, Not Never	69
Woman, What Is Your Worth?	71
Prayer Works	72
Bless Yourself Always	73
Can God Use Me?	74
Fruit	75
Poisons & Antidotes	77
Mirrored Image Of Hotel	78
The Enemy Wears Sheep Clothing	79
Bragging Rights Are Wrong	81
Life's Highway Lanes	82
Dreams Unrealized	83
Motivation Above Suppression	85
Remember	87
Relationships – To Give Or Not To Give	88
About the Author	91

Do Not Worry

"When you see people talking about you don't worry

It means you are at the Top

When you are at the Top, you become the Topic

When you are the Head, you become the Headlines

Don't worry what people are saying behind your back

The reason they are talking behind your back

Is because they're already behind you."

P.D. MEADE

INSPIRE ME: *A Book of Odes and Things*

INSPIRE ME
A Book of
Odes and Things

P.D. MEADE

P.D. MEADE

Introduction

Over the years I have encountered many things, have suffered many things, and have had good and bad experiences at many levels in my life. But, there is one important thing, and I sincerely mean this, there is nothing that compares with having a close and personal relationship with our Savior, Jesus Christ. No matter what we go through, He carries us through. There is nothing too big for our Lord, nothing.

This book is a collection of Holy Spirit inspired writings, endowed upon me spiritually, over time. Some people put confidence in material things, superficial celebrities, or they simply have the wrong ideals on life, and how they should live it.

"Some trust in chariots, and some in horses, but we trust in the name of the Lord."

Psalm 20:7 (NIV)

I hope this book will inspire you as you read it, as it did to myself when I wrote it. Blessings!

Dedicated:

To my husband Rudy, son Ian, Daughter Madonna, grandchildren, parents, siblings, and our blended family.

Bibliography:

Book content includes: bible scriptures (from the KJV, New KJV, NIV, the Amp Bible), God inspired writings, and life experiences.

What's In Your Speech?

I sometimes feel that people and their speech, in any situations or trials in their life, have a disillusioned concept of what is real and what is unnatural. They speak and act in the natural, not in the spiritual. The Word tells us to "walk by Faith, not by Sight." As humans, we always want to take the easy road, and get into our feelings about everything. If God wanted us to literally take everything, and anything as we perceive it, in the natural, He would not have even sent His only begotten son Jesus Christ, who took on our iniquities, and bore every sin we ever committed, and be bruised for our transgressions. He would have simply allowed the enemy to rule. Not! You see, He loves us that much, that He had compassion on us all, our Jehovah Jireh, our Provider.

God loves us, even when we do not even love ourselves. Wake up people, stop mirroring your life after empty wishes, fake fetishes, worldly impressionists. The Lord loves you just the way you are. After all, He knew us all, before we were a sparkle in our parents' eye, he knew us, before we were knit in our mother's womb.

He knows us all by name and nature, but has no respect of persons. Whether you have a CEO position or a Garbage truck driver, you will be judged by Him, on that day. As the song that "When the saints go marching in . . . I want to be in that number . . ." I often say to myself, that I do not want to have the wrong thoughts before I leave this earth, I pray that Lord will always let the words of my mouth, and the meditations of my heart, be acceptable in Thy sight, O Lord my strength and my Redeemer. Amen!

My mother always told me that, it's not the food that we eat that defiles us, but the words that comes out of our mouths. The book of Matthew 15:17-20 tells us . . . " [17]Do you not see that whatever goes into the mouth passes into the stomach and is expelled? [18] But what comes out of the mouth proceeds from the heart, and this defiles a person. [19] For out of the heart come evil thoughts, murder, adultery, sexual immorality, theft, false witness, slander. [20] These are what defile a person. But to eat with unwashed hands does not defile anyone."

What's In Your Spiritual Wallet?

Is it KINDNESS, LOVE, UNDERSTANDING, LONGSUFFERING, or just Bitterness? Empty that wallet of those worldly pennies of discontent, and keep those "Bills of PEACE."

The Bible tells me to LOVE my enemies, and that I should turn the other cheek, so to speak, if others come at me the wrong way, that other cheek is Humility, and I should not render evil for evil no matter what trials come. You see, as believers, we do not have Haters, but Destiny Admirers. I know I have been changed.

"What's in your spiritual wallet?"
Keep praying and believing that all of God's promises are for real, and more precious that anything this world has to offer.

Prayer Is The Key That Unlocks All Doors!

Daniel 2: 21 (KJV)

²¹ And he changeth the times and the seasons; he removeth kings, and setteth up kings: he giveth wisdom unto the wise, and knowledge to them that know understanding;

We serve an all knowing, all seeing, all powerful God who loves us and has redeemed us through the blood of Jesus. He knows our plights, past and present. After all this world will pass away in His time, He has control. Trust Him.

Internalized Slavery

Neither dressing up in an ancestral outfit, or speaking the language of your forefathers, will not transform you into an acceptable person, it is a mere illusioned expression, and delusion of worldly grandeur.

Instead, put on the robe of righteousness, so that the Lord, can present you faultless before the presence of the Most Holy God.

We are all precious in God's eyes, all the time, not just once a year. Discrimination is not just a black or white issue, it's an issue of ignorance, an issue against a people, whose outward appearance may not mesh with the so-called generalized society. The only standard that God requires of us, is that, we love Him with all our minds, strength, and soul, and, that we should love our neighbor, as ourselves.

Life in this world is like a chess game, we have to choose whom we serve. Are we going to be pawns or seek after the Savior. He alone open doors no one can close, and shuts doors, no one can open. Knowledge is power. We are more than conquerors.

Do not be taken captive due to prideful ambitions. In all relationships, be slow to anger, and be quick to forgive. We fool ourselves when we keep hold of old hurts. We become prisoners of our unforgiveness, and unrepented sins. Do not internalize, be transformed by the renewing of the mind.

Remember, as we read in Proverbs 16:32 (KJV)
[32] He that is slow to anger is better than the mighty; and he that ruleth his spirit than he that taketh a city.

The Emperor's New Clothes

This story is about an emperor who was sold a magnificent set of clothes by two swindlers. The swindlers claimed that the clothing is invisible to anyone stupid or incompetent while they pretend to weave and sew using empty looms and needles.

It took a young boy to point out the truth "the emperor is naked."

The moral of the story is. If we don't stand for something, we'll fall for anything.

Be wise, not foolish.

Victorious Life

"What's in your Spiritual Wallet?"

Is it:
* DECEPTION
* SELFISHNESS
* UNFORGIVENESS
* MALICE
* GREED
* VANITY
* PRIDE

"What does it profit anyone to gain the whole world, and lose their own soul?"

"Man cannot serve two masters"

Where do our loyalties lie?

Is it conforming or transforming?

Are we God chasers, or people pleasers?

Or, are we running for a corruptible crown?

Choose ye this day whom you shall serve!

What Do You Live By?

5D PRINCIPLES:

*DESIRE	- Be actively involved in reaching goals
*DETERMINATION	- Keep moving forward
*DISCIPLINE	- Loyalty is the key
*DEDICATION	- Keep your mind staid on what is right.
*DEVOTION	- Keep on keeping on.

*THESE ARE FUNDAMENTALS TO ACHIEVING POSITIVE END RESULTS IN ALL THAT YOU DO.

The Tabernacle Is Not Just A Building
The Tabernacle – Our Secret Place

Your secret place should be a place of hope, of peace, of rest, of faith.

We are the TABERNACLE of the Holy Spirit. We cannot get to the most holy place in communion with the Father if we don't put on our new garment of faith, trust and obedience.

My take on all this pandemonium is: God allows things to happen, as with Job, in the Bible, who lost everything, but, he did not curse God.

This time allows all of us to have clarity in how we were living, and, how we should be living. Maybe the worldly idols, we were holding onto, the green grass on the other side was just a mirage of non-essential worship.

ALSO,

I do not feel that we should have favorite children, grandchildren, family or friends, yet, God wants us to be discerned. He said "choose you this day whom ye will serve . . . (Joshua 24:15)"

Why I'm saying this is, because I see this in my own family. And, I also see a so called "trickledown effect" because, when you really think about it, if any of our siblings impart certain ways i.e. selfishness, tunnel vision, isolation, disconnection, egotism, we know that DNA is in effect.

That's what I feel. We are Non-PERFECT. We were all flawed from the Garden of Eden. We are a rebellious people. The Bible tells us that "the content of a man's heart is evil continually."

(Genesis 6:5)

This is 2020, the year of CLARITY. The year of REVELATION.

That is why God is giving us this 'shelter in place' moment to reposition ourselves, pray, meditate, and come back to Him.

That's my view.

Family First

It should not take a pandemic to happen for us to LOVE each other, show respect to one another, put aside grudges, and FORGIVE each other, as God forgave us, when He sent Jesus Christ His only begotten son, to this earth to deliver us and cleanse us on the CROSS AT CALVARY. How can we say we love God who we cannot see, and HATE our brother and sister who we can see daily? That means we lie, and the truth is not within us. Love is the greatest and most powerful gift God gives us, from the very beginning. Let us be wise, and strive to do His perfect will, for we are NOT PERFECT.

John 3:16 is the greatest Word ever. Be blessed.

Praise Break

PRAYER

Lord God, My Father, strengthen this bond of Love between us. Deliver me from temptations, and help me see that your Love, your light, is the only my salvation and soul depends on. Release me from worldly sins and wicked possessions, from the sea of lust, pride and distraction, to purify my soul Lord, which I wIsh only to bring us closer to you and your infinite embrace.

Amen.

B.E.L.I.E.V.E.

BELIEVE TO RECEIVE AND

RECEIVE TO BELIEVE

FEELING INADEQUATE IS CAUSE FOR UNBELIEF

"I CAN DO ALL THINGS . . . . . . "

GET the Word DREAD out OF your vocabulary, BELIEVE, "I CAN DO ALL . . . "

Have a CAN DO attitude.

FAITH LEADS

MANIFESTATION FOLLOWS

BUT FAITH LEADS

FIGHT THE ENEMY WITH YOUR SWORD

OF TRUTH

AS LONG AS YOU KEEP BELIEVING, GOD KEEPS WORKING . . . 'ALL THINGS ARE POSSIBLE TO HIM THAT BELIEVETH.

Mark 9:23

READ Mark 9 Entire.

Joshua 1:8 Meditate

MEDITATION IS positive worry

Worrying is negative meditation

What's Going On?

Does anyone ever wonder why we are going through BLOODY times. Those who believe know we are in the last days of time. The book of 1 Peter tells is 'Be alert and of sound mind. Your enemy the devil prowls around like a roaring lion looking for someone to devour.

I do not even need to talk about the relentless shootings and murders going on every day. I do not even look at the news too much, but, the Lord wants us to be informed. but, not consumed or conformed by the ways of the world, but we should be transformed by the renewal of our minds.

There are many who are of an abased mind right now, thoughtless of what is spoken, careless in their doing. My Lord.

PRAYER CHANGES THINGS. Like in the book of Esther, we need corporate prayer to save our world.

We as a people don't always want to hear words like these, but, we have to utilize our discernment, in these times.

We have to guard our spiritual Gates, our Mouthgate (spoken words) our Eargate and Eyegate (what we listen and focus on).

We are God's children, we are valuable, we are all special to Him.

Remember God Loves the sinner, but, hates the sin.

How can we say we love God, whom we cannot see, but hate our brothers and sisters whom we see every day, that means the truth is not in us. (1 John 4:20)

We need renewed HEARTS. Let God break up the stony grounds within us, and replace it with Love.

Fear Not!

Those who have ears let them hear, what the spirit of the Lord is saying. Fear not.

Psalm 91 King James Version (KJV)

[1] He that dwelleth in the secret place of the most High shall abide under the shadow of the Almighty.

[2] I will say of the Lord, He is my refuge and my fortress: my God; in him will I trust.

[3] Surely he shall deliver thee from the snare of the fowler, and from the noisome pestilence.

[4] He shall cover thee with his feathers, and under his wings shalt thou trust: his truth shall be thy shield and buckler.

[5] Thou shalt not be afraid for the terror by night; nor for the arrow that flieth by day;

⁶ Nor for the pestilence that walketh in darkness; nor for the destruction that wasteth at noonday.

⁷ A thousand shall fall at thy side, and ten thousand at thy right hand; but it shall not come nigh thee.

⁸ Only with thine eyes shalt thou behold and see the reward of the wicked.

⁹ Because thou hast made the Lord, which is my refuge, even the most High, thy habitation;

¹⁰ There shall no evil befall thee, neither shall any plague come nigh thy dwelling.

¹¹ For he shall give his angels charge over thee, to keep thee in all thy ways.

¹² They shall bear thee up in their hands, lest thou dash thy foot against a stone.

¹³ Thou shalt tread upon the lion and adder: the young lion and the dragon shalt thou trample under feet.

¹⁴ Because he hath set his love upon me, therefore will I deliver him: I will set him on high, because he hath

known my name.

¹⁵ He shall call upon me, and I will answer him: I will be with him in trouble; I will deliver him, and honour him.

¹⁶ With long life will I satisfy him, and shew him my salvation.

Where To Go For Your Prayer Needs

1. When You Are Stressed

Peace I leave with you; my peace I give you. I do not give to you as the world gives. Do not let your hearts be troubled and do not be afraid.

John 14:27

2. When You Are Happy

Rejoice always, pray continually, give thanks in all circumstances; for this is God's will for you in Christ Jesus.

1 Thessalonians 5:16-18

3. When You Are Sad

He heals the brokenhearted and binds up their wounds.

Psalm 147:3

4. When You Are Anxious

Do not be anxious about anything, but in every situation, by prayer and petition, with thanksgiving, present your requests to God. And the peace of God, which transcends all understanding, will guard your hearts and your minds in Christ Jesus.

Philippians 4:6-7

5. When You Are Excited

May the God of hope fill you with all joy and peace as you trust in him, so that you may overflow with hope by the power of the Holy Spirit.

Romans 15:13

6. When You Are Discouraged

Have I not commanded you? Be strong and courageous. Do not be afraid; do not be discouraged, for the Lord your God will be with you wherever you go.

Joshua 1:9

7. When You Are Grieving

Blessed are those who mourn, for they will be comforted.

Matthew 5:4

8. When You Need Comfort

I have told you these things, so that in me you may have peace. In this world, you will have trouble. But take heart! I have overcome the world.

John 16:33

9. When You Are Scared

Be strong and courageous. Do not be afraid or terrified because of them, for the Lord your God goes with you; he will never leave you nor forsake you.

Deuteronomy 31:16

10. When You Are Insecure

"For I know the plans I have for you," declares the Lord, "plans to prosper you and not to harm you, plans to give you hope and a future."

Jeremiah 29:11

11. When You Are Lonely

Even though I walk through the darkest valley, I will fear no evil, for you are with me; your rod and your staff, they comfort me.

Psalm 23:4

12. When You Are Angry

A gentle answer turns away wrath, but a harsh word stirs up anger.

Proverbs 15:1

Essential Living

WHAT DO YOU TELL YOURSELF EVERY MORNING AS YOU START THE DAY?

- MOSES would say, "Lord . . . if You don't go with us or before us . . . we are not going anywhere."
- ABRAHAM would say, "The Lord will provide."

- JACOB would say, "I won't let go of You unless You bless me."

- JOSHUA would say, "As for me and my house . . . we will serve the Lord."

- SAMUEL would say, "Speak Lord . . . for Your servant is listening."

- NEHEMIAH would say, "The joy of the Lord is my strength."

- DAVID would say, "The Lord is my Shepherd, I shall not want and This is the day that the Lord has made and I will rejoice and be glad in it."

- SOLOMON would say, "Trust in the Lord, oh my soul, and lean not on your own understanding, in all your ways acknowledge Him and He shall direct your path."

- ISAIAH would say, "Arise and shine for my Glory has come." and "No weapon formed against me shall prosper."

- JEREMIAH would say, "The Lord has plans to prosper me and not to harm or fail me."

- JABEZ would say, "Oh . . . that you may bless me and enlarge my territory."

- SHADRACH, MESHACH and ABEDNEGO would say, "We will not bow down to any image but will serve the Lord."

- EZEKIEL would say, "Any dry bones in my life . . . LIVE AGAIN."

Choose your daily statement of FAITH . . . MEDITATE ON IT and SPEAK IT EVERY MORNING.

Old Chinese Proverbs

OLD CHINESE PROVERBS

If you build a 3 story building in an area covered with huts, you become an enemy.

If you earn more money than your friends, don't tell them.

If you have bigger plans than your friends, don't tell them.

They will hate you for it, keep your mouth shut.

Do your work in secret, and show your results openly.

Numerous friends, mean no deep friendship.

In hardship, we see true friendship.

An inch of time is worth an inch of gold, but an inch of gold may not buy an inch of time.

Without standards no boundaries are set.

Repay good with good.

Facts beat eloquence.

A good book is like a good friend.

Failure is the mother of success.

It is easy to find a thousand soldiers, but hard to find a good general.

A bad beginning, makes a bad ending.

A good name is better than a good face.

One beam, no matter how big, cannot support an entire house on its own.

You Count!

Number one in your life's blueprint, should be a deep belief in your own dignity, your worth and your own somebodiness.

Don't allow anybody to make you feel that you're nobody. Always feel that you count. Always feel that you have worth, and always feel that your life has ultimate significance.

Martin Luther King, Jr.

Nothing Heals If You Make It Fester

CHECK THIS OUT!

You know what gets me amazed, is, why do people think that it's their job to run your life, STOP, we have our own personal calendar, God controls that, we don't need earthly tour guides.

Redemption

We are all born with a sinful nature, but, through the love of God, and His only begotten son Jesus Christ, we have a promise of eternal life, once we accept Jesus as our personal savior, we can be assured of a place in heaven. Just keep doing what is right. You will know in your heart, because Jesus speaks to us and directs us from there, that's our discernment.

ROMANS 10:9

[9] If you declare with your mouth, "Jesus is Lord," and believe in your heart that God raised him from the dead, you will be saved.

Forgiveness

Sometimes we have to cease holding onto stuff or grievances in our lives. How do we expect God to bless us, if we cannot move past our hurts, forgiveness is key.

This life is fragile, we are only here temporarily, what we bind here on earth, we bind in heaven. Life was never meant to be easy. Even the bible tells us that 'the world is full of trouble.'

An ounce of prevention, is worth a pound of cure.

Jesus gave us the gift of forgiveness

During Jesus Christ's life upon the earth, he taught others, performed miracles and spread His gospel. The last week of His life, He performed the greatest miracle of all, when He suffered for our sins and laid down His life.

He took upon Himself the sins of the world and suffered for each one of us. In the garden of Gethsemane, Jesus felt the weight of every sin and pain of every person who has ever lived, bleeding from every pore. He was betrayed, arrested, and crucified on the cross. This was a sacrifice only He could make, and He did it willingly because He loves us.

How does Jesus's sacrifice affect my life?
We all make mistakes we cannot fix, experience losses we cannot recover, and face pain and disappointment that we can't handle alone. Because of Christ's sacrifice we don't have to.

He helps me to forgive
Jesus commands us to forgive those who wrong us. It may be very difficult to forgive others that have hurt or offended us, but when we ask for help, Christ can give us the strength to overcome feelings of anger and

bitterness.

He helps me to repent

Jesus has the power to forgive completely. When we repent and rely on Him, we will become clean again.

He helps me be stronger

Jesus Christ loves us and wants to help us. Through His grace, we can receive divine help or strengthening to do things that we would not be able to do on our own.

He understands completely

Because Jesus Christ suffered for all of our sins and pains personally, He knows us perfectly. He loves us and want us to rely on Him through trials and hardships. He knows exactly what we are going through and knows how to help us.

Difficult Circumstances Releases Courage

COURAGE

"The ability to do something that frightens one"

Matthew 5:13-16 (NLT)

¹³ You are the salt of the earth. But what good is salt if it has lost its flavor? Can you make it salty again? It will be thrown out and trampled underfoot as worthless. ¹⁴ You are the light of the world—like a city on a hilltop that cannot be hidden. ¹⁵ No one lights a lamp and then puts it under a basket. Instead, a lamp is placed on a stand, where it gives light to everyone in the house. ¹⁶ In the same way, let your good deeds shine out for all to see, so that everyone will praise your heavenly Father.

L.O.V.E.

NO HEART - NO LOVE

NO LOVE - NO CONSCIENCE

NO CONSCIENCE - NO COMPASS

Dear family,

I know a lot of us say we know God, but do we? We have to recognize that these 'perilous' times are not by chance, but by prophecy. It's not G5 that we should be concerned with, but, getting back into a true relationship with God. We, including myself, have allowed 'worldly' pleasures to motivate our daily lives, leaving out grateful worship. We cannot just talk the talk, but walk the talk. The "jezebel" spirit is real, and has caused a lot of hurt to families, marriages etc.

As the song says 'back to life . . . etc.' we need to go back to God.

God is our EOP (Equal Opportunity Provider) He has no respect of persons. He is healer for myself, you, and everyone who calls on His name. Prayer works.

God does not give us the spirit of fear, but, He wants us to be wise, not foolish.

Be safe.

Special Words

Waiting on God is an important spiritual discipline in our walk of faith. King David's life teaches us about the value of following the Lord's plan and the danger in moving ahead of Him.

When David was a young shepherd boy, the prophet Samuel anointed him as Israel's next king. Yet he did not become the ruler for many years. Waiting for the Lord to place him on the throne was made more difficult because the current king, Saul, turned against David and repeatedly tried to take his life.

Despite the opportunity to take matters into his own hands and kill his enemy, David held back. He wouldn't allow anyone else to attack Saul either (1 Sam. 24:1-7). He waited on God and was greatly blessed for his obedience.

King David also knew what it was like to move ahead without the Lord. One year he chose not to join his troops in battle, even though that was one of his duties (2 Sam. 11:1). During the time he stayed home, he noticed Bathsheba, the wife of Uriah, and he coveted her. Acting upon his desires, he conceived a child with her and then tried to cover up his sin. What a mess he made of his life. Instead of following the Lord's plan and being blessed, he experienced divine chastisement and much heartache.

As believers, we want to obey the Lord, but there may be situations when intense desire propels us forward without waiting for His direction. Like David, we will experience the blessing of obedience or the heartache of disobedience. Be sure to seek out God's plan before you act.

Bless Yourself

We need to bless ourselves always, make it a daily habit, and say to yourself daily.

In Christ I am happy

I am protected

I am guided

I am healed

I am healthy

I am strong

I am loved

I Am Blessed

It truly makes a great difference when we speak positivity in our life.

During the year 2020, we have seen many challenges, many griefs, many unresolved issues. But, we only have to take that leap of faith, and be encouraged, that everything that occurs in our lives, are seasonal. There is a time for everything under heaven.

Remember, an ounce of prevention, is better than a pound of cure, always.

The biggest problem is not dying from a virus.

The BIGGEST problem is dying without Jesus Christ.

Playing For Keeps

Just imagine if SALVATION was a Game, how many would WIN or LOSE?

Some may be playing with a full deck, others, with a partial one, or not quite playing with a full one.

It is said that we have to play the hand we are given, without cheating, or swopping out.

As a people, why do some feel they have the monopoly on life, or the need to call other people's shots, when all they need to do, spiritually, is, pray and seek God's guidance.

After all, He is the WAY, the TRUTH, and the LIFE.

Remember, Facebook is the World's platform, where some positive posts may be LIKED or DISLIKED, but, I refuse to be deterred by anything.

We all have a FREE WILL, it's on what path we choose

to Walk down. I hope you choose John 3:16 as your first response, not your last resort.

Sweet Honesty

HAVE YOU HONESTLY LOOKED AT YOURSELF TODAY?
AND WONDERED WHAT OTHERS MAY HAVE TO SAY
DO YOU REALLY CONSIDER THEIR QUESTIONS AND VIEWS?

AFTER LISTENING TO PONDERINGS AND PROCRASTINATIONS, YOU WONDER TO YOURSELF, . . .TO ME THIS IS JUST PLAIN OLD NEWS . . .

WHAT A FEELING TO BE IN ONE'S OWN REFLECTIVE STATE

IRREGARDLESS OF THOSE WHO FAIL TO COMMUNICATE

MANY HAVE BEEN BORN, AND MANY HAVE PASSED ON, THEIR PAST IMPRESSIONS LIKE BLOWING GRAINS OF SAND

DOES ANYONE CARE ENOUGH TO STOP, STAND THERE, REFLECT, AND SMELL THE AROMA OF SWEET HONESTY!

What A Surprise

ISN'T IT SOMETHING THAT PEOPLE CAN TELL BOLD FACE LIES WITHOUT BLINKING.

WHAT A TRANSPARENT WORLD WE LIVE IN.

HOW YOU ASK?

ANSWER: SPIRITUAL OMNISCIENCE. GOD SEES ALL.

Destiny

Thoughts of possibilities, never afar,

endless speculations overtaking mentality.

Decisions, conditions, considerations, conclusion.

Succession destined . . . . Destiny sublime.

Jamaica

Sunshine blazing over shores of bronze and blue

bodies loungin, surfing, memories renewed

"Whaapen Man! take a dip with me na"

"Tek it eazy, you de pon vacation"

Sipping fruit punch, over crushed ice,

soothing on SP15, "bway dat feel nice"

Soon vacation time escapes into blue mists

orange sunset, purple morns,

gazing over landscape up above so high,

Descending over green,

grey,

back to dismal reality . . . .

Someone Like You

Eyes so brown, gleaming with positiveness

Mentality overflowing, dreams being fulfilled

Waves of emotions meaningfully challenged

Love yearning renewal development, revival

Is this you?

I watched you walk into a room

eyes capturing glances, yet unknowing

Is love what you're searching for?

Man Of My Dreams

Man of my dreams

Man of my semi-consciousness

Who are you? where are you to be located?

Are you for real, or part of the imaginary mind?

It would be wonderful to be near someone like you . . .

Imagine

Wonders always cease to amaze

The Lord never ceases to inspire

Imagine His near presence

How wonderful is He

Always knowing our innermost thoughts,

our innermost desires.

Even before we ourselves can begin to contemplate

how.

He Is our All, He is our everything.

We can only imagine,

yet, we know His greatness and Power is neverending.

God Is Real

When you add up the Pros and Cons in your

relationship with God

It is without doubt, He is what He says

He is always there for us in all our troubles.

We ride storms together, or alone

He is always there beside us, footprints in the sand,

taking us along, one step at a time,

through tribulations of our life.

Allowing us to be aware, that we are infallible.

Never expect everything to be just so,

be still,

let the beats of your heart remind you,

that God is REAL.

Prayer For The World

I pray that God gives us all the Grace and Peace we need right now, to take us through these perilous times. We need it. Read the book of Esther. Corporate prayer is essential, now. Not only for us individually, but, for the nation, the world.
Amen.

SO TRUE

"Family will come miles to bury you, but would not cross a street to come support you."

(Unknown Author)

NO TIME FOR GOD?
WHAT IF GOD HAS NO TIME FOR YOU?

GOD WITHOUT MAN IS STILL GOD!
MAN WITHOUT GOD IS NOTHING
(Read John 15:5)

SOMETHING

IT SOMETHING THAT PEOPLE CAN TELL BOLD FACE LIES WITHOUT BLINKING.

WHAT A TRANSPARENT WORLD WE LIVE IN. HOW YOU ASK?

ANSWER: SPIRITUAL OMNISCIENCE. GOD SEES ALL.

THIS IS WHO WE ARE

We are the TABERNACLE of the Holy Spirit. We cannot get to the most holy place, and be in communion with the Father, if we don't put on our new garment of faith, trust and obedience.

BE EDUCATED

Do something, follow something, but cannot spell 'something' isn't that SOMETHING!

Reading is Fundamental.

WHERE ARE YOU GOING?

WE ARE LIVING ON A SPACESHIP CALLED EARTH, DESTINATION UNKNOWN, IF YOU ARE NOT PREPARED.

Who Matters?

Truth is ALL OF US MATTER.

From birth, from an African heritage standpoint, we supposed to dedicate our children to God. What a lot of us has done is to leave 'caution to the wind' expecting our children to choose their spiritual way, when they come of age. Sorry, it is already too late then, their minds are already abased. Wake up people. God is real, He knew us before we came into being.

Stop!!!

We need to cease holding onto stuff or grievances. How do we expect God to bless us, if we cannot move past our hurts, forgiveness is key. Come on now. This life is fragile, we are only here temporarily, what we bind here on earth, we bind in heaven. Life was never meant to be easy. Even the bible tells us that 'the world is full of trouble.' We cannot follow our mother's mindset, you see what mess we're in right now. Sorry to say, but true.

NO WHAT?

NO HEART - NO LOVE
NO LOVE - NO CONSCIENCE
NO CONSCIENCE - NO COMPASS

A Little Tidbit ... Enjoy!

ANTIVIRAL TEA

GARLIC
GINGER
LEMON
CINNAMON
TURMERIC
WATER

Put all ingredients in a pan, and boil for about 15 minutes on a moderate setting. Cool and serve.

MAKE A BATCH & STORE IN JAR/PLASTIC CONTAINER IN REFRIGERATOR. DRINK SHOT GLASS FULL DAILY.

GREAT ENHANCEMENT FOR THE LUNGS, AND THE LEMON HELPS WITH THE ALKALINE NEEDED FOR THE BODY.

PLUS, PLACING A FEW SLICES OF FRESH LEMON OR LIME IN YOUR WATER, JUICE OR TEA IS SUPERB. YOU GET A DOUBLE DEAL. NOT ONLY ARE YOU ALKALIZED, YOU GET VITAMIN-C AS WELL.

Overwhelming Grace

There are many who labor only for recognition.

There are some that labor for self-esteem.

But, the few, who gives of their best, does it selflessly.

God Graced us with Love, the only thing that is lasting

The best legacy left behind you,

Is that you bind all to heaven, by giving your best on earth.

*Dedicated to Evon Jones - RIP March 2021.

Impacted Journey

What will you do to impact somebody's life today?

What is your impact on daily living?

Will you forward bless somebody today?

This world is only a temporary sitting place.

Do not get too comfortable in that rented chair.

Wake up, stand up and see, that we are mere nomads

travelling a road with two different paths.

One leading to sorrow,

The other to Life Eternal.

The only items to place in our suitcase are,

Your garments of praise and righteousness.

"Be anxious about nothing, but in everything, by prayer and supplication, with thanksgiving, let your requests be made known to God."
Philippians 4:6-7

Make It Now, Not Never

Since we were children, we were taught the scriptures,
we were told that there was no other way.
But, now we're much older, and very much seasoned,
we can now see, no other direction is purposed entirely.

Make it now not never, come to the Master.
Give your life over to the Lord!
Tomorrow, may be too late.

Make it now not never, Yeshua is King!
Now that we are in these days and times,
where we see life, is only a vapor.

There is no tomorrow, as it is not promised,
Seek the Lord today, for there is, no other way.

Make it now not never, come to the Master

Give your life over to the Lord!

Tomorrow, may be too late.

Make it now not never, Yeshua is King!

Woman, What is Your Worth?

Woman,

    You are worth more than GOLD

Woman,

    You are the Mother of Invention

Woman,

    When you Weep, God Hears clearly

Woman,

    You have Purpose

Woman,

    You were created from the rib of man,

    but, you are the source of *The Human Race*

Woman,

    Know your worth

Woman,

    Keep on soaring higher, and higher.

        God knows your Worth!

Prayer Works

(Job 22:27-28 AMPC – *Amplified Bible, Classic Edition*)

²⁷ You will make your prayer to Him, and He will hear you, and you will pay your vows.

²⁸ You shall also decide and decree a thing, and it shall be established for you; and the light [of God's favor] shall shine upon your ways.

Bless Yourself Always!

Say daily . . . .

In Christ . . . . I am Happy

                I am Protected

                I am Guided

                I am Healed

                I am Healthy

                I am Strong

                I am Loved

I AM BLESSED!

Can God Use Me?

Many have pondered on whether you are good enough for God to use them. Do not be dismayed, yes He can. Throughout bible history He has blessed and allowed many to do His will, even though those folks were none perfect, like all of us.

For example:

NOAH	got drunk
JACOB	lied
MOSES	murdered
RAHAB	was a prostitute
DAVID	had an affair with a married woman

God still used them. He can use you too.

God is a gentleman, He does not push you to know Him, He invites us into building a relationship with Him.
Just as We Are.

Fruit

Let's take a piece of fruit, let's say an orange. It may look good from the outside, but peel and squeeze it, taste it, and you will surely see whethere it's sweet or sour.

The same can be said of some believers. They look good on the outside. They could also say "I'm saved and sanctIfled, filled with the Holy Ghost."

But, you squeeze them the wrong way, and see what flavor you will get. It could seem that you were in the company of sailors. I am not saying that all sailors are colorful, I love our military servers. But, you don't always get what you see in any person. Looks are truly deceiving sometimes.

Hence the saying, "You are known by your fruits."

Be sweet in this life. Put away bitterness, unforgiveness, malice or envy, which imprisons. Let us give each other sweet smelling roses, pay kindness forward, with love.

Poisons & Antidotes

With every poison the enemy has for us, God has the antidote.

Poison	**Antidote**
You are defeated	I can do all things through Christ who gives me strength. - Phil. 4:13
When arrows (trouble) comes	Put on the Whole Armor - Eph. 6:11
Resist the enemy	Submit yourselves, then, to God. Resist the devil, and he will flee from you - James 4:7
Stay in Peace at all times	No weapon formed against you shall prosper - Isaiah 54:17
Lying thoughts; Don't give up	Casting all your cares upon him; for he careth for you - 1Peter 5:7

Mirrored Image Of Hate!

Hate - Such a strong word. A deep dislike. An ignorance.

We all belong to the Human Race. "For God so loved the World . . ." He loves ALL, not just one part. If one part is so hated, what is the point of being.

We are a body of people, who operates together. Every part of a body is necessary. What one does cruelly against another, reflects a mirror image of hate.

Who do you see in the mirror?

The Enemy Wears Sheep Clothing

Sometimes we close our earthly eyes to potentially damaging liaisons, knowing full well that it was not a thought out plan. Open those spiritual eyes, look and discern your betterment. Do not be led astray by mere travesties.

Why do we as human, discredit ourselves, our worth, our being, and foolishly settle for crumbs under the table? Instead of waiting on our Father, the King of Kings to render us a full plate of desired delicacies, at His table.

Are we so blind, so impatient, so shallow, that we are willing to settle for measly bowls of gruel?

Wake up dear friends! You are depriving yourselves of

true enlightenment, and true grandeur to living an empowered lifestyle.

You were created from Love, and that Agape love allows much overflow, which transcends all.

Bragging Rights Are Wrong

There are some boastful people who like to brag about their luxury, blessings, and materialistic things in front of others.

Be not self-absorbed or insecure.

One can be seen as an 'have it all' person, but are so very empty and unhappy inside.

It is just not worth it.

Life's Highway Lanes

Speaking about LANES. Be careful of stepping into someone else's domain.

Jesus is our highway pass to Heaven.

All other lanes help to get us to that main route, but we have to employ caution in using those side roads, lest we become distracted or meet upon roadworks, or adverse diversions, which can throw us off track, in reaching our desired life goals.

So, be diligent, keep in the Word, which is our GPS to everyday living.

Dreams Unrealized

Let me ask you this question. How many of us have had dreams, as a child, which did not take root? I am certain they could be . . . "I did."

Sometimes, as a parent we fail to recognize potential in our young. During what we call the 'old days' - there tended to be so much fear of the unknown, so to speak. And, because of this mindset, we, and our offsprings can potentially miss out on this possibility of dreams realized, by us, but, unrealized by others.

I remember at the age of about 11 or 12 years of age, during the late 1960's, I had aspirations of being a dancer, but, because of fear of the unknown, that dream was squashed.

In fact, a dance scout visited our family home one day, but, my parents, due to fear, and lack of knowledge, they quickly turned down that proposal of me being a protege. That door of opportunity quickly faded. I am not blaming my parents, because it may not have been the right time for this. Only God knows.

We still have to walk by faith, not by sight. God opens doors to us, and sometimes, we, or others involved, can allow them to slam shut.

No matter what disappointments we may face in life, we should never stop exploring, and reaching our potential.

Realize, and act on your dreams, because, with God, all things are indeed possible.

Motivation Above Suppression

We all experience life in different ways. Some of us may have underwent physical trauma, or indeed mental oppression, and, not always at the hands of strangers. Rarely, do we give our attention to the ones who are truly going through traumatic issues, instead, we are always ready to weigh wrong judgements, or cast untrue assertions, of why he or she is acting in a way not conducive of their true self, and is somewhat misinterpreted as, and portrayed to be 'not normal' behavior.

Actually, what is 'normal?' Is it normal to be hateful? Is it normal to mistrust others? Is it normal to do the wrong thing?

The world's ideology of normalcy does not correspond with God's Word, or God's Way.

Do not allow the negativeness of this, sometimes cruel world, to interfere with our blessed gifts of the spirit. We must continually strive, to motivate our brothers and sisters, especially, those who clearly are walking through traumatic paths, and get rid of their suppressive blankets, and replace that oppressive covering, with Divine Love.

Lastly, and with a disclaimer of the following prose:

"We make a living by what we have,

and

We make a life, with what we Give."

Remember

You can be whatever you want to be.

The only person to believe in you------is yourself.

God knows you were a successor from before you were born.

Always know that you are:

* A Victor
* An Overcomer
* You are the Head, not the tail.
* You can do all things through Christ who strengthens you.

Relationships – To Give Or Not To Give

In any relationship, if one is part of a couple or a team, not only one succeeds, all succeed.

Yet, some people will say, that as a couple, you should equally put in 50%, each, to make 100%.

Not. That is incorrect.

You see, whether it's the male, or the female, it does not matter who brings in the most. For example, one could bring in 70%, and the other 30%, it still amounts to 100. That it my analogy, you may not agree.

"For better, or for worse," is a vow, during the wedding ceremony, that you both agreed upon, for your marriage, right.

But, we, in this world get so caught up with status, and are much to hung up with 'who gives how much.'

It is a real shame, that we, as a people, can be so shallow and underserving, in how we respond to each other, or how we show gratitude in everyday life.

In any family unit, like a marriage, we ideally should be helpmates, not help weights.

About the Author

My name is Patricia Meade, Author of "*Beyond Belief, Two As One*" an autobiography of my life, spanning over three countries. I was born in Kingston, Jamaica, in 1953. Emigrated to London, England in 1962 during British colonialism. Becoming a British Citizen in 1963.

I obtained all my education through school and college, and university studies. I worked in Local

Government, and Further Education teaching establishments.

I moved to Columbus, Ohio, USA, in 1991, where I worked in the Probation System for 14 years.

I am now residing in Fort Lauderdale, Florida. Have lived in the states since 2006 to date. Now retired from the Court System.

www.ingramcontent.com/pod-product-compliance
Lightning Source LLC
Chambersburg PA
CBHW070649050426
42451CB00008B/325